# APPLEKID'S CHAPTER BOOKS

*AppleJack*
*"I Like Math"*

*"Everywhere I Go"*

**WRITTEN AND EDITED BY SHERRY MCGEE
ILLUSTRATED BY RICHARD M. JOHNSON IV**

Cover Design by Richard M. Johnson IV

Copyright © 1999, Apple Book Center Stores, Inc.
All rights reserved. Published by Apple Book Center Stores, Inc.
The AppleKids are trademarks and/or registered trademarks of Apple Book Center Stores, Inc.

Library of Congress Catalog Card Number: 99-096323

ISBN 0-9673591-2-0

Printed in the U.S.A.
First Printing, November 1999

*The AppleKid's Chapter Books are dedicated with love to children, families, and communities everywhere.*

# Chapter 1

Hello boys and girls. My name is AppleJack. I'm one of the AppleKids. Do you know the AppleKids? We're just a bunch of normal kids who really like school. We all have our favorite subjects. I like math. Do you want to know one thing I've learned about math? It's everywhere I go.

You see, I like to find ways to practice math outside of school and homework. Sometimes when I'm just daydreaming, I find ways to practice my math. My grandfather tells me all the time that because I like math so much I can be anything I want. A pilot. A physicist. Even an economist. I'm not completely sure what they all do, but I know they all have something to do with math because my granddad says so. He's the greatest.

My granddad taught me something about math I'll never forget. It's about interest and compounding. My grandfather likes to take life easy. He's retired now. He says it's the happiest time of his life because he has a lot less to worry about and he can spend more time with me. My granddad says it's all because he started saving early and let his money grow with interest and compounding.

# Chapter 2

One weekend my granddad and I were just chilling out together and he showed me how saving money works. He said if I save just $5.00 from my allowance each month, at eight percent interest I would have almost $1,000 to use for college. Wow!

As soon as I went home, I asked my dad to take me to the bank to start my own savings account. We went early Monday morning. Ever since then each time I get my allowance, I set aside some money for fun stuff, some money for things my sister asks me for and I put the rest into my savings account. My dad says I'm going to be just like my granddad... very comfortable when I get older. My dad says he has the same kind of savings plan for college for my sister and I. I guess that's why we're a family. We all think alike.

Now about my sister. Her name is AppleJill. She really likes science. She likes it so much that she's always finding things and bringing them home like rocks and insects. My mom doesn't mind. She encourages us to explore things. AppleJill always needs more money because she buys all this cool stuff for experiments. She borrows a lot of money from me. Sometimes I say to myself, "Self. If that wasn't your sister, do you know how much you could earn in interest on the money she's borrowed?" I would never charge my sister interest but I can see how having money can help you make money.

# Chapter 3

Banks and other places that lend money charge interest. That means you pay back what you borrowed plus extra. The extra amount that you pay back is called interest. There are companies that are in business just to loan money. This is what people mean when they say "money makes money". If you're watching and listening, you'll notice money being loaned all around you. Math is everywhere!

One holiday, my mom was the host for the family dinner. She asked my sister and I to set the table. We were expecting 25 guests for dinner. So, we needed more than one table. We set a smaller table for the really little kids and used the big table for the adults. My mom said to use the good dishes. There were 12 adults coming. For each adult we needed 5 pieces of silverware, 2 plates, 1 bowl and 1 glass. To make sure we had enough dishes before we left the kitchen, we did the math. 12 times 5 for the silverware. 12 times 2 for the plates and 12 times 1 for the bowls and the glasses. Can you tell how many of each we needed? It's just math.

During dinner, my mother's cousin announced that she's getting married. We were all happy. She wanted to wear my mom's wedding dress which is a size 8. I heard my mom ask her how could she wear a size 8 in six months when right now she's a size 16? My mom said her cousin would have to loose quite a few pounds. I volunteered to do the math but my mom smiled and said, "Sssh. Never mind you." "Oh, well" I said. "It's just math."

# Chapter 4

I've even found ways to practice my math at the grocery store. My dad and I go to the grocery store once a week usually on Saturday morning. Dad lets me calculate some of the prices to practice my math. I can tell him how much we're going to spend on meat by calculating the price for each pound. My dad will say, "The price per pound is 69 cents. We're getting 3 pounds son." Then I do the math. Three times 70 cents per pound is $2.10. We round when we're not using a calculator. I can tell him how much our fruits and vegetables will cost. And, sometimes I can almost calculate how much our bill will be and how much change we can expect. That's a lot of math.

One Saturday, my friend AppleNeil went to the grocery store with us. AppleNeil loves to tell a good joke. He said he made up some math jokes just for me. He said, "AppleJack. Do you know why you shouldn't do math in the jungle? Because if you add 4 + 4 you get 8. Get it? You get ate!" Then he said, "AppleJack. Do you know why 6 was afraid of 7? Because 7, 8, 9." We both laughed. AppleNeil is my good friend. He's cool.

My dad's brother owns his own company. His name is uncle Benjamin. His company prepares income taxes. He showed me how easy some of the forms can be because they involve just doing math. Last year, he taught me how to complete what's called the *Short Form*. He showed me where the numbers come from and where they go on the form. Then, I just do the math. It's kind of easy. We went to our neighborhood bookstore and I found several books that would help me learn more about money and math. Uncle Benjamin helped me earn enough money to upgrade my computer with a faster modem. I had asked my mom for the money first. Here's what she said.

# Chapter 5

When I asked my mom for some extra money, the first thing she said was, "Why do you need more money?" I told her that the modem on my computer was outdated. I needed to upgrade to a faster modem. One that would work better on the Internet and with my computer games. Then she said I should save for it. When I asked her how long would I be saving she said, "I don't know. Just do the math." So I did.

A new modem would cost $75.00. I figured I'd have to earn some extra money since I was already saving money from my allowance. That's were uncle Benjamin helped. As long as I finished the things I was responsible for at home including my homework, I could help uncle Benjamin around the office. He gave me $25.00 a week. I had the full $75.00 in just three weeks.

My mom said she was real proud of me. She said now I have my new modem and I know more about responsibility. I knew she was teaching me some kind of lesson. Parents have a way of showing you important things like that. It's cool.

# Chapter 6

The thing about math is whether you're at home, at school, or just out and about, math is everywhere. I'm glad I like math because I can help my sister and others with things that require math skills. Do you like math? It's good if you do. It's OK if you don't. Just know that math is everywhere you go too.

## The End

*Knowledge is power.*
*Reading is one of the easiest ways to acquire knowledge.*